FUN to LEARN
Science

Graham Peacock
Illustrated by Jean White

Educational Advisory Panel

Bernard Ashley – Head teacher and author

Diana Bentley – Language adviser

Peter Patilla – Lecturer and author

Susie Sainsbury – Nursery teacher

WALKER BOOKS

AND SUBSIDIARIES

LONDON • BOSTON • SYDNEY • AUCKLAND

Notes to Parents

Science is all around you: this series of books encourages children to look around and observe how things work in the pattern of normal life. Each page offers an activity that can be carried out from the illustration with a minimum of equipment. To children, each one is fun to do and to share; for parents there is the reassuring knowledge that the activities are worthwhile and that they reinforce the children's work at school.

In order to help your children:

* talk through the activities and listen well to their responses

* encourage them to talk about the pictures as much as the science involved

* talk about different approaches to each question, rather than imposing one method of working

* praise them frequently

* don't do too much in one session, but let them return to the pages they enjoy most

Notes on the educational purpose of each topic are listed below, with a reference in brackets to the specific subject area covered.

1   Faces
(Genetics)
The main idea on this introductory page is that people vary a great deal. Play the game where you pick one of the faces in the illustration. Children have to guess who it is by asking questions. Then swap over.

2   Body parts
(Processes of life)
Naming parts of the body.

3   Joining parts
(Processes of life)
Naming the body's main joints. These are rotating joints like the hip, and hinge joints like the elbow. You could talk about the joints you can twist. Where can you feel your bones beneath your skin?

4   Body covering
(The variety of life)
There is a huge variety of living things. Skin is covered in a wide range of materials. Birds are unique in having feathers. Snakes and other reptiles are dry and scaly. Slugs and snails are slimy partly to help them glide over rough ground. They leave a trail of slime behind them. People have some hair like most mammals.

5   Animal parts
(The variety of life)
Animals have an enormous range of limbs and other body parts. Animals can do a variety of things. You could ask more questions which encourage closer observation of the pictures, such as:
Which animal has a beak?
Which animals have long claws?
Which creature can swim?

6 Animal homes
(The variety of life)

The underground animals are the mole, worm and rabbit. The rabbit's hole and the molehill are visible. In the tree you can see the blue tit's nesting hole and the squirrel's untidy drey. The duck's nest is by the pond. Some fish have underwater nests where they lay their eggs.

7 Making bubbles
(Types and uses of materials)

There are several different types of liquid that make bubbles. The blowing activity encourages close observation. It is fun and if you do it on the draining board there should be little mess. You can use several kinds of bubble-making liquids. Which works best? Encourage children to notice that you need to mix or agitate the water in some way to produce bubbles.

8 Using water
(Human influences on the Earth)

We use water for a variety of purposes such as washing ourselves, cleaning things and flushing away our waste. Drains take dirty water away from our homes. Where are the drains in your house? We drink clean water in many different forms. Which of the things we buy are mainly water?

9 Keeping dry
(Earth and atmosphere)

The people in the picture are using a variety of methods to keep dry. Some are more effective than others.
Ask your child: Who do they think wasn't expecting rain in the picture? Which is their favourite waterproof coat? Which are their best rainy-day shoes?

10 Dress for the weather
(Earth and atmosphere)

Match the weather conditions to the clothes suited to the weather.

11 Dress for the season
(The Earth in space)

The weather changes as the seasons change. Living things, including people, respond to the changing seasons. People's clothing changes. Animals, like ducks, for instance, breed in the spring. Many trees drop their seeds in the autumn.

12 Push or pull
(Forces)

A force can be a push or a pull. Getting dressed and undressed involves both pushing and pulling. Talk about this, next time children get into or out of clothes. Ask children to try to push a piece of string.

13 Food and energy
(Energy)

Food gives us the energy we need to be active. When we move quickly we use lots of energy and eventually become tired. Ask children about any energetic things they have done today.

14 Signals
(Using light)

Matching colours and understanding the significance of red danger signals and green go signals.

1 Faces

Look at all these children's faces.
How are they the same?
How are they different?

What colour is your hair?
What colour are your eyes?

2 Body parts

Can you name these parts of your body?
Which ones can you find on the dog?

Can you name these parts of your face?
What is each one for?

3 Joining parts

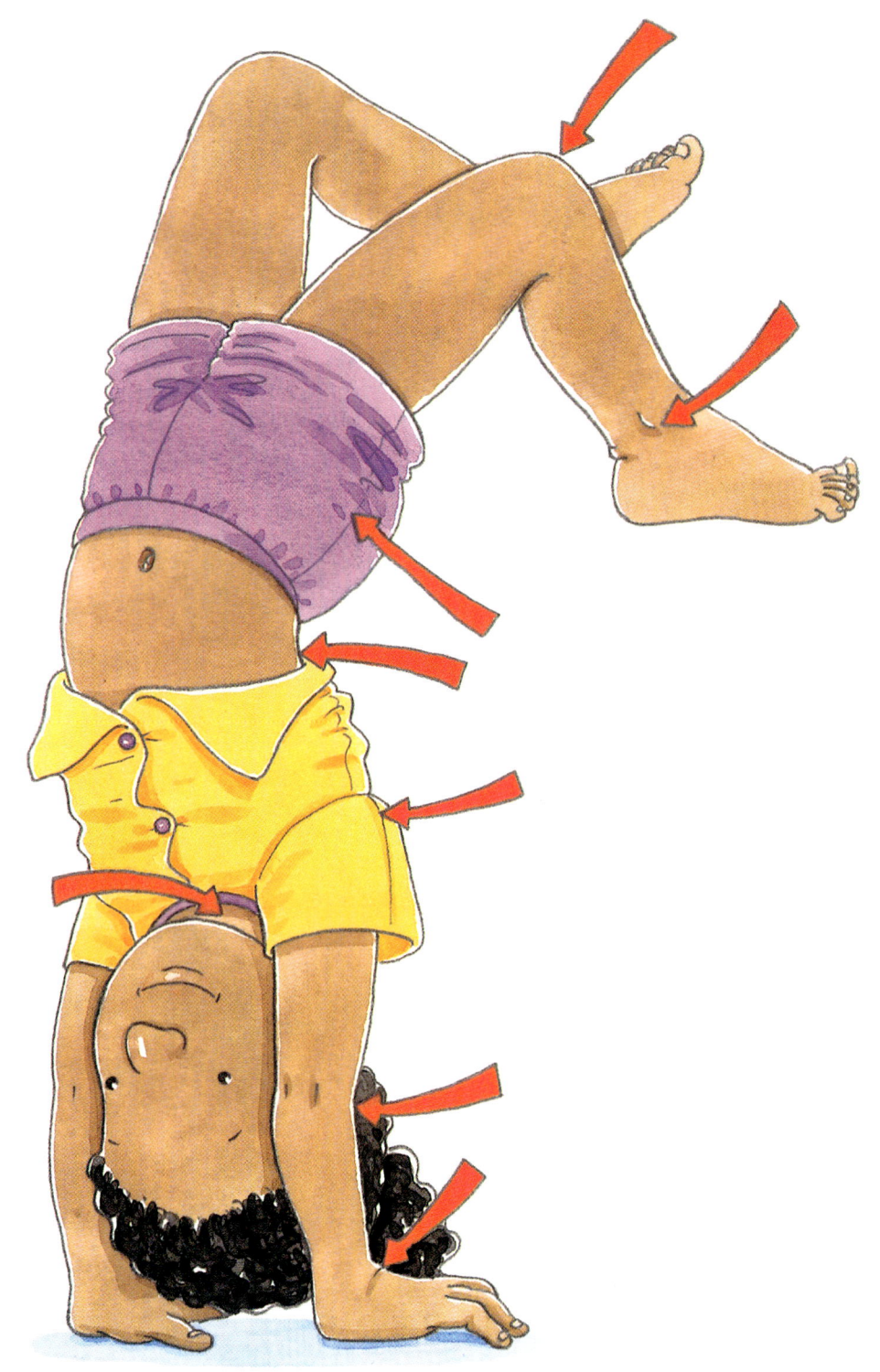

Try bending in all these places.
What does each bending part help you do?
What would happen if you couldn't bend?

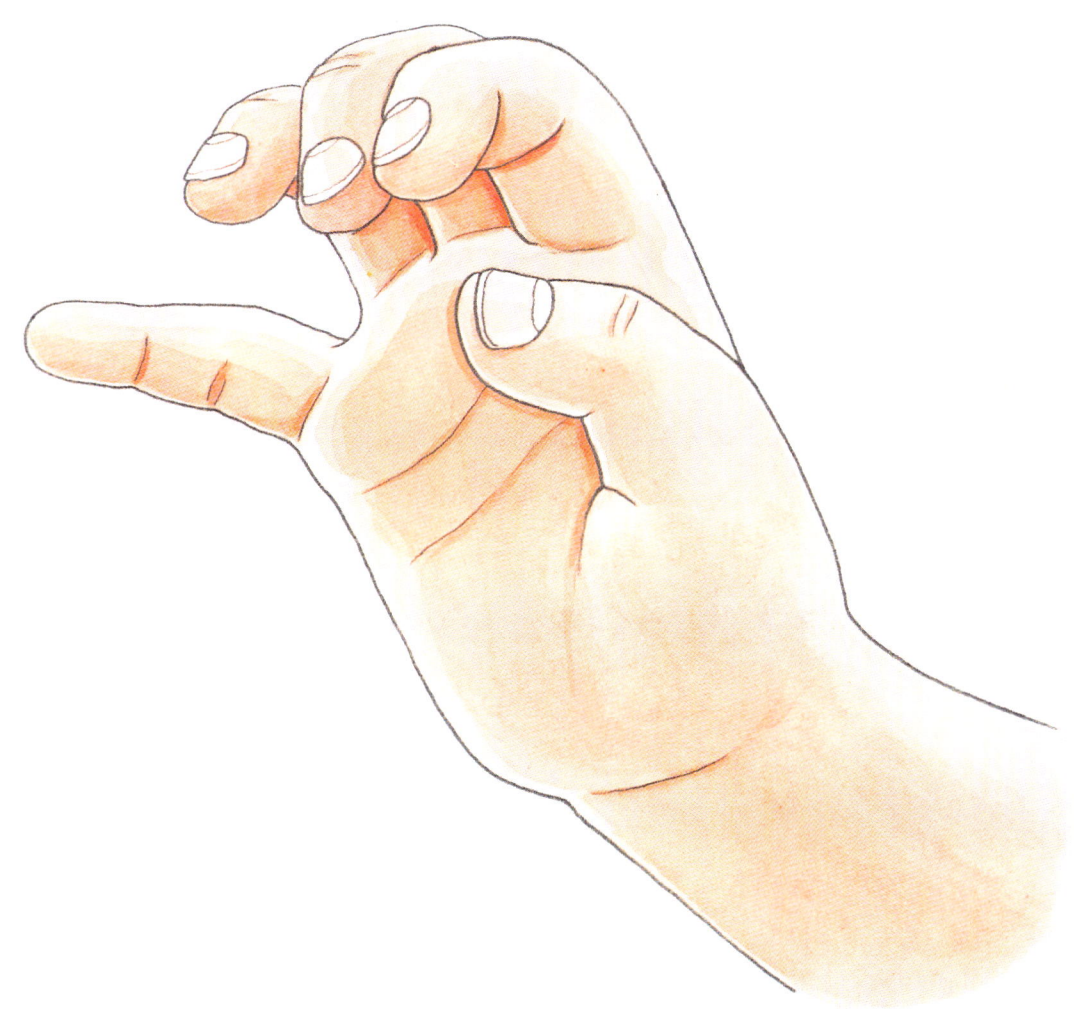

How many bends are there in each finger?
What about the thumb?
Bend yours and see.

4 Body covering

Which animals are covered in feathers?
Which animals have hard, dry coverings?
Which animal is soft and slimy?

Which animals have hair or fur?
What about you – do you have hair too?

5 Animal parts

Which of these animals can fly?
Which has a forked tongue?
Which can draw pictures and talk?

Which part belongs to which animal?

6 Animal homes

Which of these animals live in a tree?
Which do you think live underground?
Which lives near water?
Which live underwater?

Which animals' homes can you find?
Which homes are hidden?

7 Making bubbles

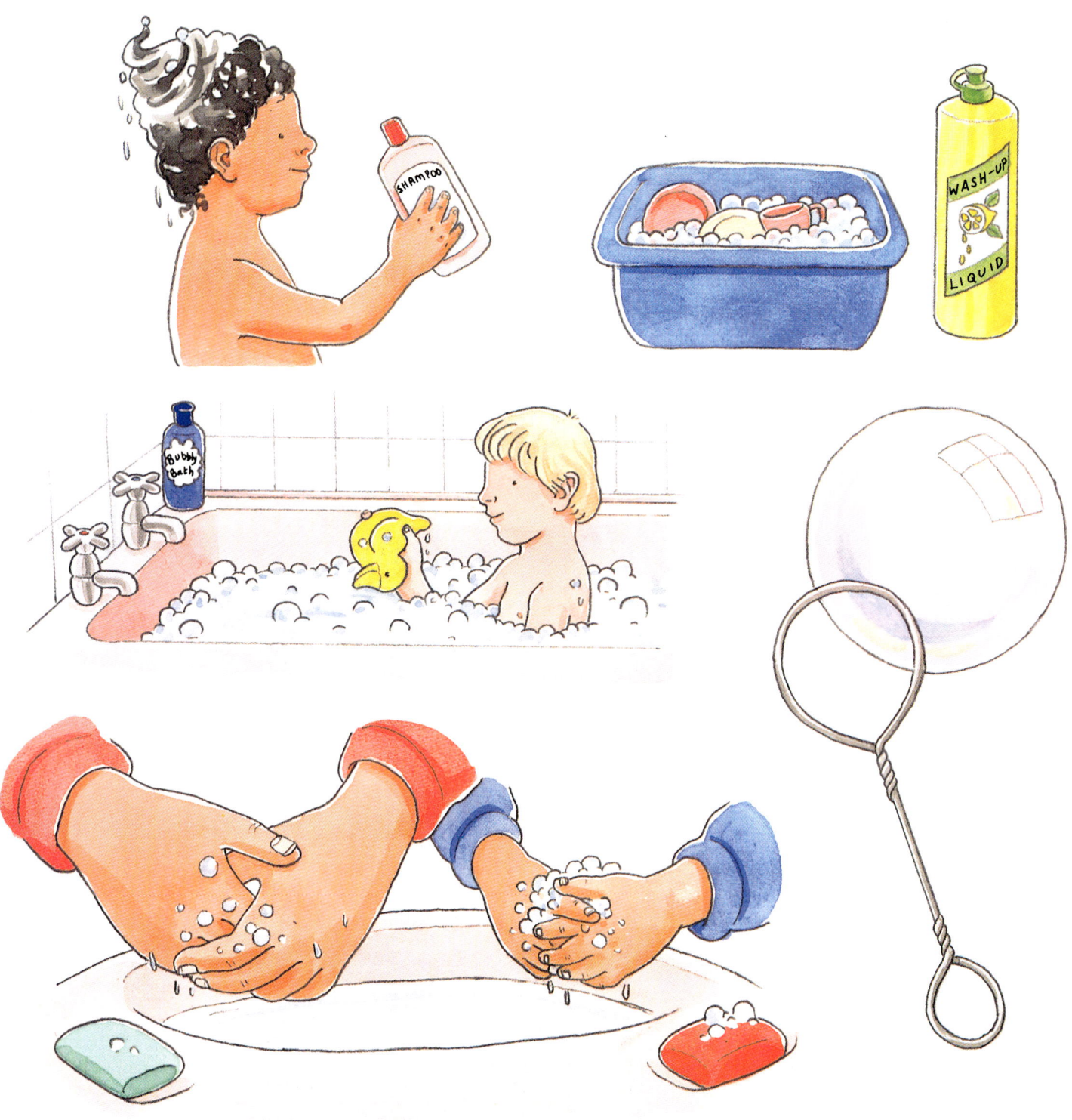

What makes bubbles and lather?
Some soap makes more bubbles than others.
You could test two different kinds.

Put two drops of washing up liquid in
half a glass of water.
Blow into the water using a straw.
What shape are the bubbles?
What colours can you see?
What happens where bubbles join?

8 Using water

Which of these things give you clean water?
Which things take dirty water away?

We use water in many different ways.
How many ways have you used water today?

9 Keeping dry

How many ways of keeping dry can you find?

Where is all the rainwater going?

10 Dress for the weather

Which pictures show warm weather?

Which picture shows cold weather?

Which picture shows wet weather?

Point to the clothes the children might wear in each kind of weather.

11 Dress for the season

Which season is shown in each picture?
What are the children doing in each season?

What sort of clothes are the children wearing?
In each picture can you spot the person who isn't
dressed for the season?

12 Push or pull

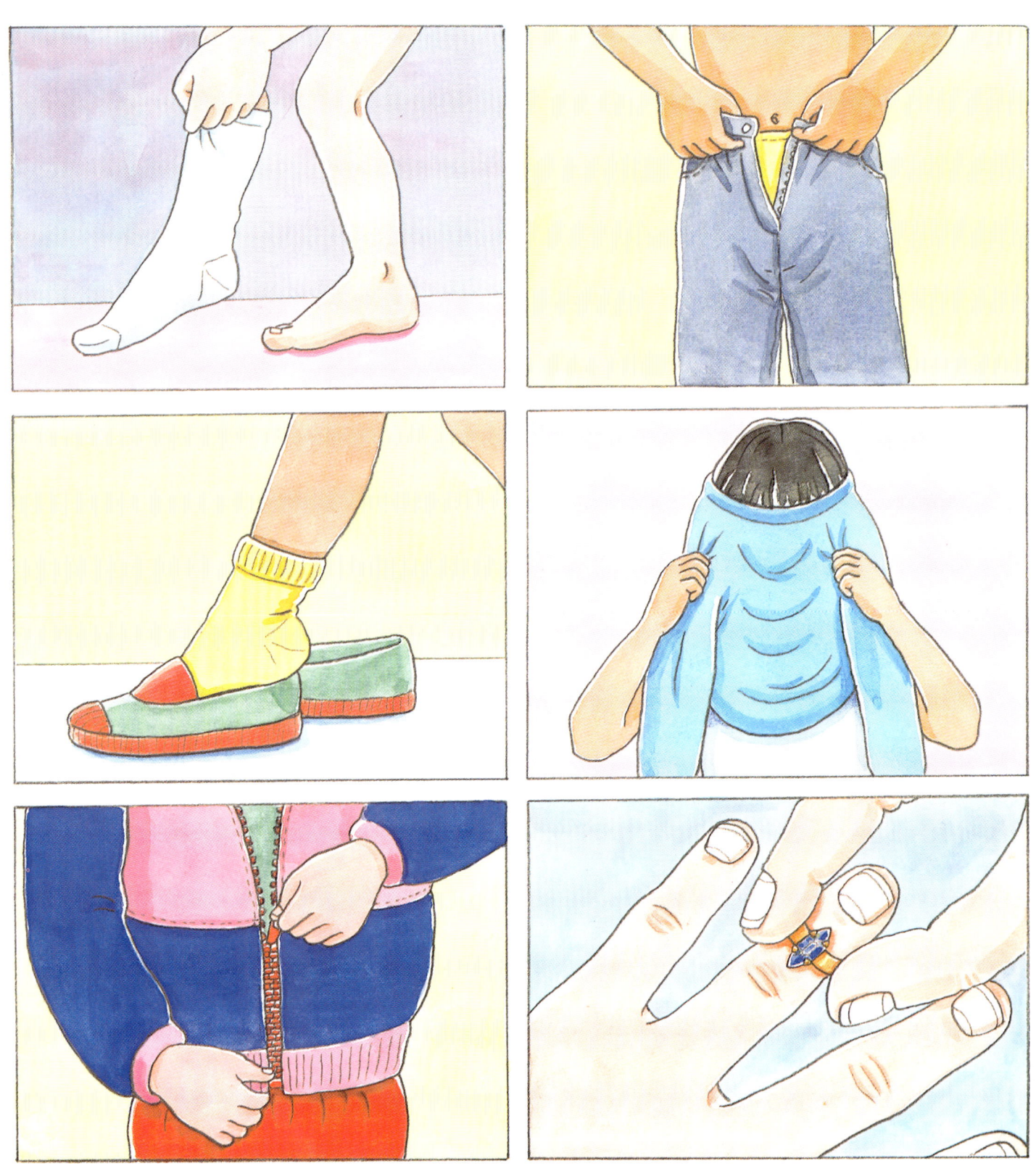

Which pictures show pushing?

Which pictures show pulling?

Which could be either?

Which toys would you push?

Which would you pull?

Which light switch would you pull?

Which needs to be pushed?

13 Food and energy

Food gives you the energy to do things.
Which of these pictures show people using
lots of energy?

Look at these pictures of a child's birthday.
Can you find people using energy?
Can you find people eating to get more energy?

14 Signals

What colour signals tell you to stop?
What colour signals tell you to go?

Here are some signs and signals.
Which ones use lights?

First published 1990 by Walker Books Ltd
87 Vauxhall Walk, London SE11 5HJ

This edition published 2003

10 9 8 7 6 5 4 3 2 1

This book has been typeset in Rockwell Light Educational

Printed in China

British Library Cataloguing in Publication Data:
a catalogue record for this book
is available from the British Library

ISBN 1-84428-805-6

www.walkerbooks.co.uk